Contents

Chapter 1
What is a Web Page?

The World Wide Web

The World Wide Web, or simply the Web, is by far the most exciting part of the Internet. It is a place where there is an amazing amount of fun to be had and educational things to do. For example you can:

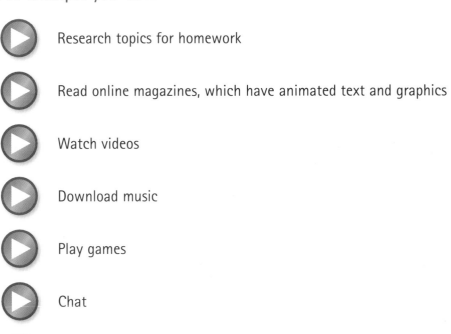

- Research topics for homework

- Read online magazines, which have animated text and graphics

- Watch videos

- Download music

- Play games

- Chat

- Buy books and CD's online!

- Visit other people's Web sites (your friends' or a star's)

The Web is very enjoyable and interesting, and you can be a part of it. The places on the Web where the information is shown are called Web pages - colourful, animated places where you can find exactly what you want. It is very easy to make your own Web page, and this book is designed to help you through the process. It will help you understand how to plan, design and produce your Web pages.

Examples of Web pages

There are thousands and thousands of Web pages to browse through. To look at Web pages, you need to be connected to the Internet, and have a Web browser such as Internet Explorer or Netscape Navigator.

Take some time to have a look at other people's Web sites and decide which you find most interesting:

 Click the Internet Explorer icon to start up Internet Explorer. ———

 Log on to the Internet.

 In the Address box, type www.nasa.gov and press Enter.

This will take you to what is known as the home page of NASA.

Figure 1.1: The NASA home page

Tip:
To find a Web site, you need to know the Web site's URL. This stands for Uniform Resource Locator which tells you exactly where the Web page can be found (the Web site address).

3

Links between Web pages

A number of pages make up a Web site. The pages on a site are joined together by hyperlinks. You can also link your pages to other people's sites. These hyperlinks can be either words or pictures.

For example, let's go to the BBC home page and look at their hyperlinks.

In the Address box type www.bbc.co.uk and press Enter or the Go button.

This will take you to the home page of the BBC.

Figure 1.2: Hyperlinks on the BBC homepage

Text hyperlinks to other pages

Tip:
Each Web site has a unique address - **.co.uk** shows that it is the address of a UK company. International companies often end in **.com**. Other codes used in Web addresses are **gov** for government, **org** for organisation and **ac, ed** or **sch** for a college or school. Web sites belonging to different countries end in a different code - **de** for Germany, **fr** for France etc.

When you move the mouse pointer over a hyperlink, the cursor changes shape from an arrow to a pointing finger.

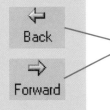

You can use the Back and Forward buttons in Internet Explorer to move to previous screens that you have viewed.

Search Engines

If you do not know a Web site address, you can search the World Wide Web using a search engine. This allows you to type in a word or phrase and it then comes back with a list of related Web pages. You will be using a search engine later on to search for some pictures to insert on your Web pages.

Note:

Some popular search engines can be found by going to the following sites:

www.yahoo.com
www.altavista.com
www.hotbot.com
www.google.com

Building a Web site

In this book we are going to use Microsoft Word 2000 to create Web pages. Most schools use this software for word processing, but there are now additional features which allow you to create Web pages very easily.

Why build a Web site?

There are many reasons for building a Web site. You can:

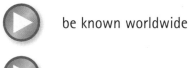 be known worldwide

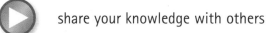 make friends with other people

share your knowledge with others

support a cause

You could base your Web site on yourself or your family, giving people information about your hobbies and favourite things. You could base your site on your school, and your school life. You could include a gallery, with pictures taken from around the school. You could also include pictures of the staff, and special educational occasions.

You could also base your Web site on your favourite pop group, or celebrity. This could contain information, pictures, and perhaps sound clips about your subject. This one is about the footballer Michael Owen.

Note:

These are not official sites - that means that the celebrity has not given their permission. Most stars have their own official site, containing more accurate information

Figure 1.3: A Web site about Michael Owen

There was only one team in the whole universe for Robin... the 'mighty' Ipswich Town!

Chapter **2**
Planning your Web Site

Before you start creating your Web site, you should first think carefully about why you are making it. Knowing the purpose of your site will help when you start designing it.

In this book you will develop Web pages for Terry, a pupil at Wilmington High School, starting with his home page. This is the page that visitors reach first and they can then access all the different areas of the site. The home page should describe what the site contains and provide links to other pages.

The Personal Web Page template

You will be using a template in Microsoft Word to create your home page. You need to know what this will look like, as it will influence your planning. Therefore, we are going to open Microsoft Word, open a new document using the Personal Web Page template and take a sneak preview of the possibilities.

Tip:
A template determines the basic structure for a document and contains document settings such as page layout and styles.

To open Microsoft Word:

 Click on the Start menu button.

 Click on Programs.

 Click on the Microsoft Word icon.

You should see the following screen:

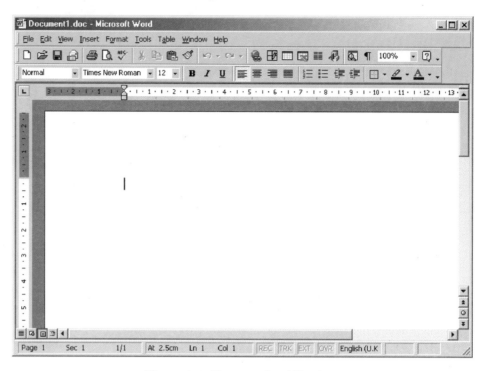

Figure 2.1: The opening Word screen

Word 2000 has a special template called the Personal Web Page template for creating personal Web pages.

To start a new Web page using this template:

 From the File menu select New.

 Click on the Web Pages tab and select the one highlighted in the figure below (Personal Web Page), and press OK.

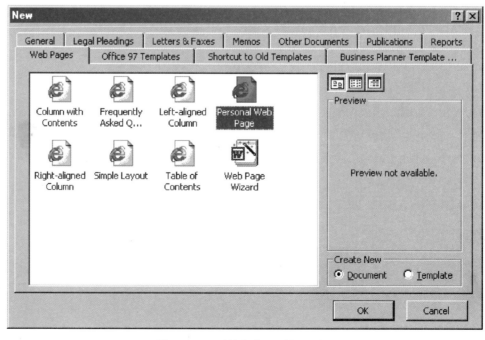

Figure 2.2: Web Page Templates

A home page will automatically be created for you, and it is ready for you to edit with your own personal information.

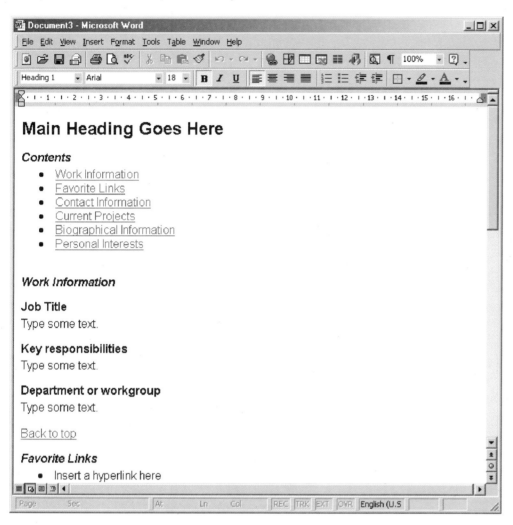

Figure 2.3: The home page ready for editing

At the top of the page, there is a Contents list, showing all the sections in the document.

 Scroll down and find the sections on Biographical Information and Personal Interests.

 Scroll back up to top of the page to the Contents list.

Notice that the Contents list is shown in blue, underlined letters, indicating that the words are hyperlinks. These words are a certain type of hyperlink, called bookmarks, which link you to a different place on the same page.

Click on the Personal Interests bookmark to be automatically taken to the Personal Interests section of the page.

 Click the Back to Top bookmark to return to the top of the page.

You could print out the document and use it to plan your home page. Below is an example of Terry's planning.

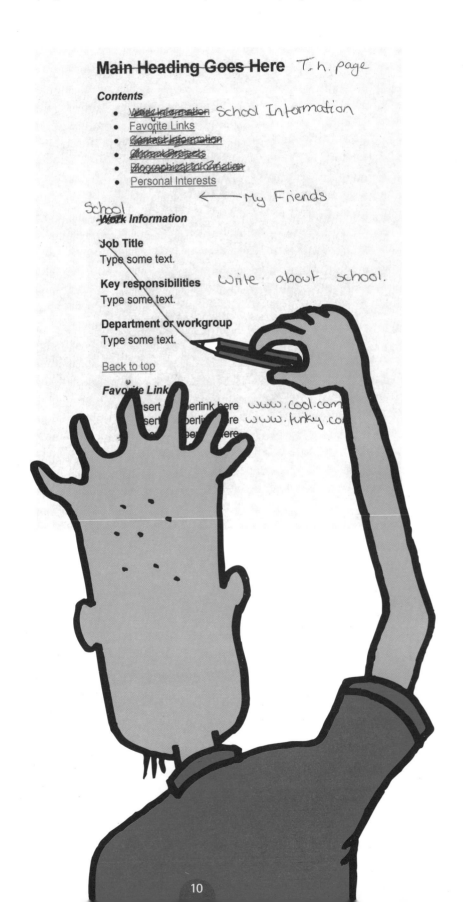

It is important to give some thought to the other pages that you want to link to from your home page. Later you will create 3 more pages, one for each of Terry's personal interests – films, music and sport. It is at this stage that you would jot down ideas for the content and layout of the pages, together with a sketch of how the links between the pages would work.

You shouldn't make your home page too crowded. It can go beyond the bottom of one screen, but try not to make your visitors scroll down more than two screens for each page. If you have too much information, you should split it into different pages and link them together.

Chapter 3
Creating a Home Page

Now that the planning and designing is complete, it's time to start creating the Web site.

 Open Microsoft Word.

Open a new document using the Personal Web Page template as described in Chapter 2.

Applying a theme

The page looks rather boring. You can make it look more interesting and eye-catching by applying one of the themes available in Word.

From the Format menu click on Theme. The following list of themes is displayed.

Note:

A theme is a set of unified design elements and colour schemes for your Web page such as background images, bullets, fonts and horizontal lines. A theme helps you to create a well-designed, professional-looking Web page.

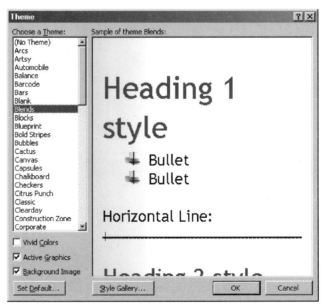

Figure 3.1: Choosing a theme

Click on a theme and you will see a preview in the right hand panel. I have chosen Blends, but you can choose whichever you prefer.

 Make sure you have selected the other options shown in Figure 3.1.

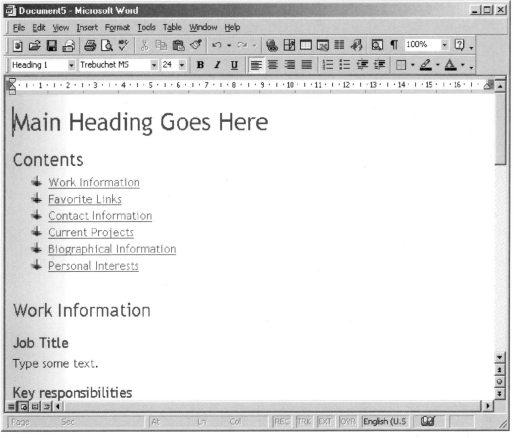

Figure 3.2: The Themed Page

Tip:
Different themes produce different styles of horizontal lines – you can try inserting one by clicking on the small arrow to the right of the **Outside Border** button on the Formatting toolbar and selecting the **Horizontal Line** option.

Customising the Web page

After you have selected a theme and applied it to your page, you need to edit the placeholder text that has been inserted as part of the Personal Web Page template. There are a number of different headings describing different things, and it is your job to edit both the heading and the content of each section.

 Highlight Main Heading and replace it with Terry's Home Page.

 Size and centre-align the heading as you would in word processing.

Underneath the main heading you can see that a Contents list has automatically been produced. The items in the list are set up as bookmarks to other parts of the page. You can delete or edit any of these items.

Tip:
Use the **Center** button on the Formatting toolbar to centre text.

Editing the text

 Highlight the item Work Information in the Contents list and change it to School Information by typing over it.

 Then go down the page and replace the section on Work Information with School Information.

 Edit the item Favorite Links to the English spelling i.e. Favourite Links.

 Then go down the page and edit the heading for the Favorite Links section.

Deleting unwanted items

We don't need some of the suggested items in Terry's home page.

 Remove the item Current Projects from the Contents list by highlighting it and pressing the Delete key.

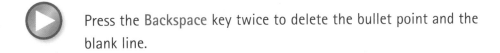 Press the Backspace key twice to delete the bullet point and the blank line.

 Then go down the page and remove the section on Current Projects.

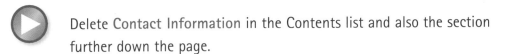 Delete Contact Information in the Contents list and also the section further down the page.

The Contents list now looks like this.

Contents
- School Information
- Favourite Links
- Biographical Information
- Personal Interests

Figure 3.3: The Contents list

Tip:
It is not a good idea to put your personal address and telephone number on the Web, because you don't know who might be reading it.

Editing the information in each section

You now need to type information into the sections further down the page.

In School Information, you can write about your school, with information about the staff, pupils' achievements and forthcoming events.

 For Terry's School Information section type in the following:

Wilmington High School
College Road
Cambridge
CB4 4YJ

1600 Pupils
Co-Educational school for 11–18 year olds

 In the Favourite Links section, insert two of Terry's favourite Web addresses so people can visit them at the click of a button.

www.cool.com
www.funky.com

 In Biographical Information type the following:

I have 7 sisters, a budgie, and a dog called Bruno.

You can make up some more information about Terry if you wish.

In Personal Interests, write:

Music
Films
Sport

You will need to delete the Back to Top bookmarks from the sections you have deleted. Delete any extra blank lines, leaving just one line between each section.

Adding a new section to the page

Terry wants to add a new section about his friends which will be called My Friends. To do this:

 Type My Friends at the bottom of the Contents list, under Personal Interests.

 Highlight the text My Friends and select Hyperlink from the Style box on the Formatting toolbar.

 Scroll down, and under the Personal Interests section, write My Friends in the style of Heading 2.

 Type on the next line: My best friends are Robin, Fee and Emma. Write a bit about each one.

Saving your work

 Select File, Save from the Main Menu.

 Create a new folder called Web Site, and save in this folder. The computer will automatically name your file Personal Web Page. You should overwrite this and name it default.

Creating a new bookmark

Now that you have created My Friends, you need to link the text in the Contents list to the actual section. To do this:

 Highlight the text, My Friends.

 From the Insert menu, select Hyperlink.

You will see this screen:

Ensure this button is clicked

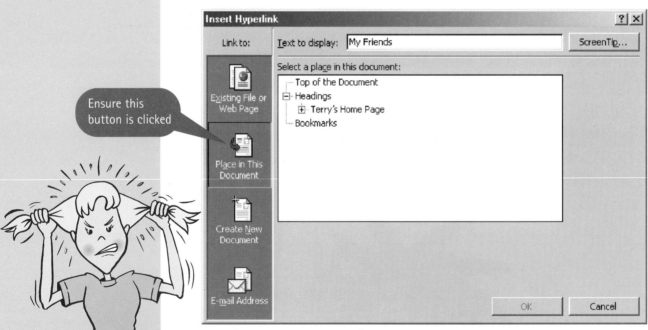

Figure 3.4: The Insert Hyperlink screen

Click on the + sign next to Terry's Home Page, and you should see this:

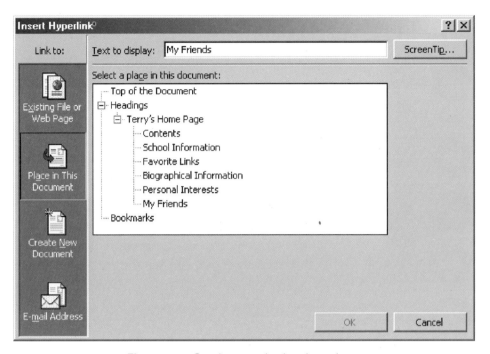

Figure 3.5: Setting up the bookmark

 Click on My Friends.

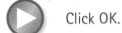 Click OK.

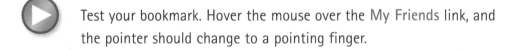 Test your bookmark. Hover the mouse over the My Friends link, and the pointer should change to a pointing finger.

Click the mouse, and it will take you to the new My Friends section.

Inserting a link to the top of the page

 Leave a line under the new text in the My Friends section, and write Back to top.

 Highlight the text and select Hyperlink from the Style box.

 Highlight the text and select Hyperlink from the Insert menu.

 Click on Top of the document; you can see the text in Figure 3.5.

 Click OK.

 Test the link by clicking on the Back to top text.

Linking to external Web sites

The addresses in the Favourite Links section have to be linked to the named Web sites. First we shall link www.cool.com. To do this:

 Highlight the www.cool.com text in Favourite Links.

From the Insert menu, select Hyperlink.

The following screen should appear:

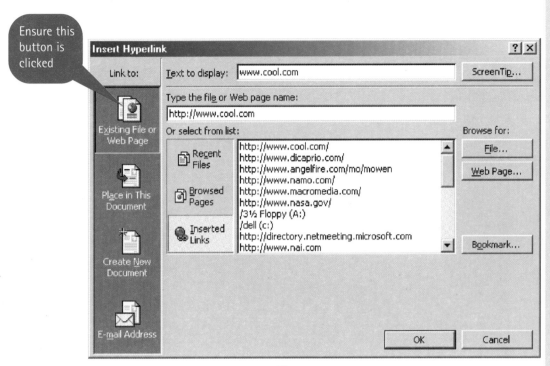

Figure 3.6

Word automatically enters the Web address.

 Click OK.

 In the same way, insert a hyperlink for www.funky.com.

The home page should now look like this:

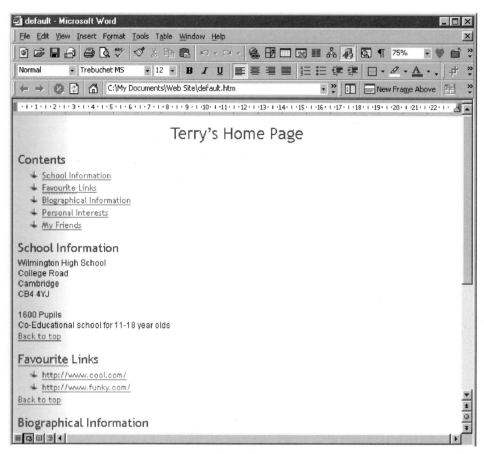

Figure 3.7

 Save the Web page.

Testing the Web page

To test the Web page, you can request a preview from within Word. This opens the page in Internet Explorer to let you see what it would look like in a Web browser.

To preview the page in Word:

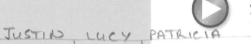 From the File menu select Web Page Preview.

Internet Explorer will automatically be opened and will display the Web page.

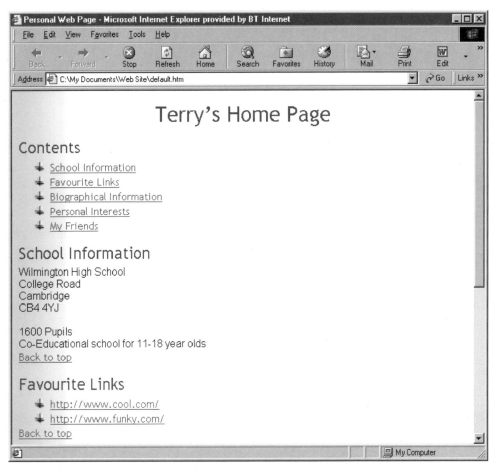

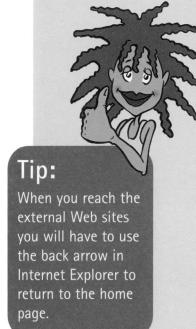

Tip:
When you reach the external Web sites you will have to use the back arrow in Internet Explorer to return to the home page.

Figure 3.8: The home page viewed in Internet Explorer

Test all of the hyperlinks. Remember the bookmark links in the Contents list should take you to another part of the page and the Favourite Links should take you to other Web sites.

Test that all the Back to top bookmarks work correctly. If there is a problem edit them as described above.

Select File, Close to close the Web Page Preview.

Back in Word, select File, Close to close the document. You can exit Word if this is the end of the session.

Assuming it all worked correctly you have now completed your first Web page. But there's lots more you can add to your site to make it more interesting, as you will see in the next few chapters.

Chapter 4
Adding Pages

In the last chapter the home page included a section on Personal Interests under which you listed three areas of particular interest to Terry. We are now going to create a new page for each of those interests and create a link to them from the home page. We must also remember to include a link on each of the additional pages so that we can return to the home page.

 From the File menu, select New.

 Click on the General tab and select the Web Page template.

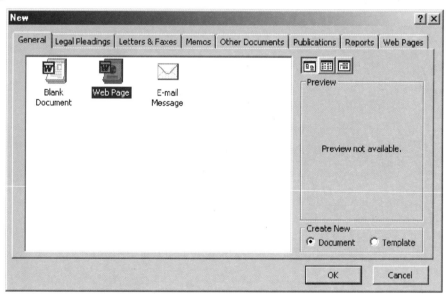

Figure 4.1: Adding a new Web page

This time you are presented with a completely blank page to work with.

 Apply the same theme as you did on the home page (Blends).

Using text styles in a theme

The theme has automatically set up certain text styles for you to work with.

 Click on the arrow next to the Style box on the Formatting toolbar and you will see them.

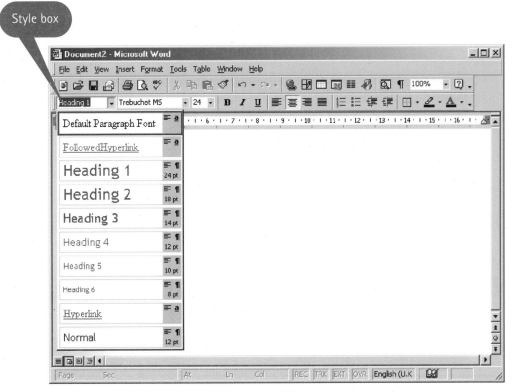

Style box

Figure 4.2: The style list

 Select Heading 1 and then type the title of your new page, Music (the first Personal Interest).

 Click the Center button on the Formatting toolbar to centre the —————— heading.

Saving the new page

 From the File menu click Save As Web Page. In the Save As Web Page dialogue box, Word will automatically name the file for you, probably Music.

 Be sure you are saving in your Web Site folder.

 Click Save.

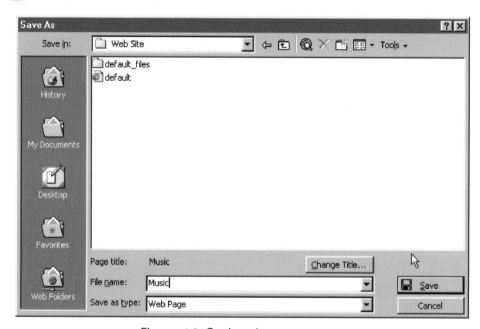

Figure 4.3: Saving the new page

Creating two more pages

Now that the new Music page has been saved, we need to add the other pages for Films and Sport. To create the new Films page:

 From the File menu, select New.

 Click on the General tab and select the Web Page template.

As before you will be given a completely blank screen to work with.

Apply the theme as you did for the home page and Music page (Blends).

Again, the theme will set up certain text styles for you to work with which can be accessed from the Style box on the Formatting toolbar.

 Select Heading 1 and type the title of your new page (Films). Centre the heading.

 Go to the File menu and click on Save as Web Page. In the filename box, Word will have automatically named the file for you.

 Click Save.

 Follow exactly the same procedure to create the third Personal Interest page (i.e. Sport). Save the page and then return to the home page.

Figure 4.4: The three new pages

Linking the pages together

You need to create links to the newly formed pages. This can be done using the same technique that we used before for creating bookmarks. However, you are about to learn a different way of doing it!

 Open the document named default which you created in Chapter 3 and saved in the folder Web Site.

 Either select Personal Interests from the Contents to follow the hyperlink or scroll down to that section.

Inserting a hyperlink

 Highlight the first Personal Interest text (Music).

 From the Standard toolbar, click on the Insert Hyperlink icon.

You will see the screen below:

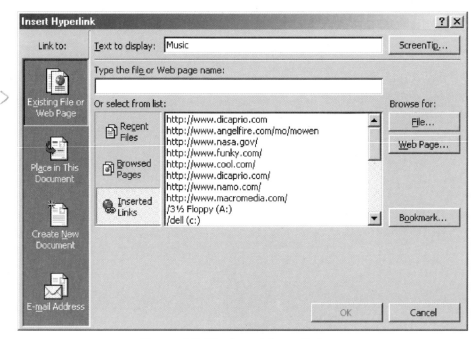

Figure 4.5: The insert hyperlink screen

On the right of the screen, you will see an option saying Browse For:. Click on File.

 Select Music and click OK.

 Click OK again.

The Music text will now be a different colour and underlined – that text is now linked to your Music page.

Linking the Films and Sport pages

You need to do the same for the Films and Sport text. For each one:

 Highlight the text.

 This time from the Insert menu, click Hyperlink.

 Click on Browse For: File.

 Select the relevant file name, and click OK.

 Click OK again.

Now the Films text will be linked to your Films page, and the Sport text will be linked to your Sport page. Save your work.

Chapter 5
Inserting Tables

Most Web pages are designed with **tables** to break the page up into different sections.

We will practise using tables on the **Films** Web page created in the last chapter. By the end of this chapter it will look like the screenshot below. We will be developing it further in Chapter 6.

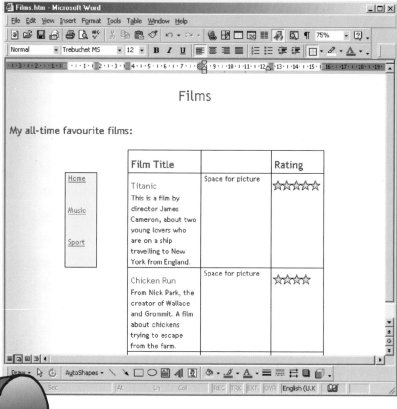

Figure 5.1: The Films Page

Further down the listings you may find a little known film 'Ted, One Man and His Bongos'. Sadly only Terry's Mum went to see it – and she fell asleep.

Creating a table

From Word, open the Films Web page which you saved in the Web Site folder.

Under the heading Films, leave a blank line and then type My all-time favourite films:. Format this as Heading 2 style.

Leave another blank line and insert a table by clicking on the Insert Table button on the Standard toolbar.

Drag across the grid to make a 4 x 4 table. A blank table is inserted into your page.

Drag the right-hand grid line of column 4 to the left so that it is half the width of the other columns as shown in Figure 5.2.

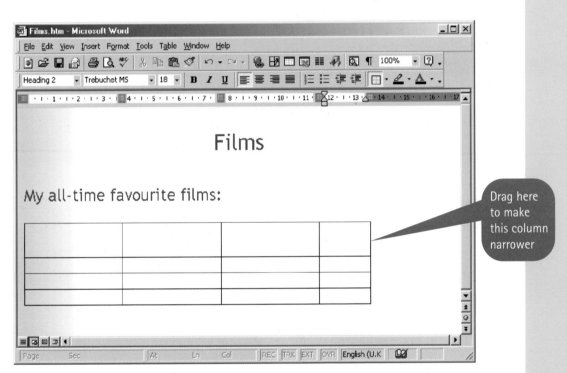

Drag here to make this column narrower

Figure 5.2: The basic table inserted on the page

Type the following headings in Heading 2 style:

In row 1, column 2 type the heading Film Title

In row 1, column 4 type the heading Rating

Changing the column width

The first three columns need to be wider.

 Highlight the first three columns.

 From the Table menu, select Table Properties.

 Click the Column tab at the top of the dialogue box.

 Enter 5.5cm in the Preferred width box.

 Click OK.

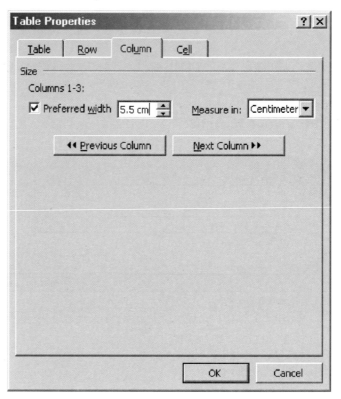

Figure 5.3: Changing the column width

Centering the table on the page

 Click anywhere in the table.

 From the Table menu, select Table Properties.

 Click the Table tab at the top of the dialogue box.

 Click the Center option in the Alignment options.

 Click OK.

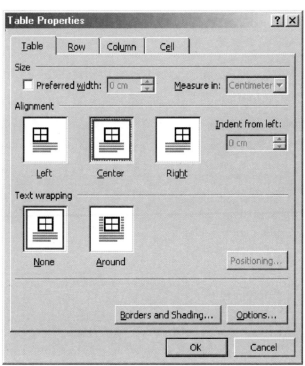

Figure 5.4: Aligning the table

 Enter some information about two films in column two.

 In the corresponding cells in column three type Space for picture.

Inserting an Autoshape

In the Rating column, we will insert a number of stars depending on how you rated the film. The Drawing toolbar needs to be visible at the bottom of your screen. If it is not:

 From the View menu, click on Toolbars.

 Select Drawing.

Now we can insert the Autoshape (a star).

 Click in the Rating cell for the first film.

 Click on Autoshapes on the Drawing toolbar.

 Click on Stars and Banners and select the last star on the top line (the five point star).

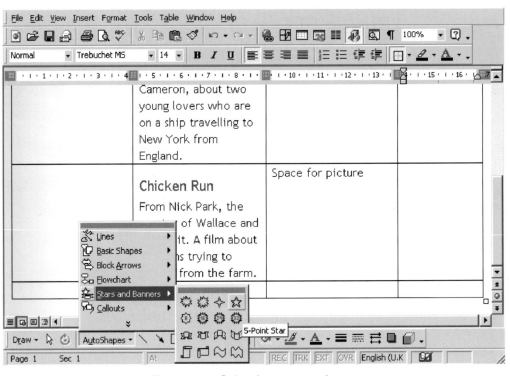

Figure 5.5: Selecting a star shape

 Drag in the cell to draw a small star.

 While the star is selected, choose a fill colour from the Fill tool on the Drawing toolbar.

Formatting the AutoShape

 Right-click the star and from the pop-up menu, select Format AutoShape.

A dialogue box appears.

 Click the Layout tab, and select In Front of Text.

Figure 5.6: The Format AutoShape dialogue box

Tip:

Holding down **Ctrl** while you drag, copies rather than moves the star. Holding down **Shift** means it can only move horizontally or vertically.

 Click OK.

 With the star still selected hold down Ctrl and Shift while you drag the star to copy it as many times as you want to show the star rating. Widen the column if necessary, depending on how many stars you are awarding!

Copying the stars to other rows

You can copy the stars to the second row for the rating of the second film, as follows:

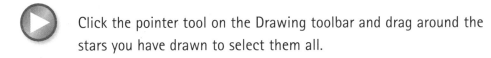 Click the pointer tool on the Drawing toolbar and drag around the stars you have drawn to select them all.

Hold down Ctrl and Shift while you drag them down to the second row.

You can use the arrow keys to move the stars with pinpoint accuracy to get them in exactly the right place.

Delete any unwanted stars to correspond to your rating of the film.

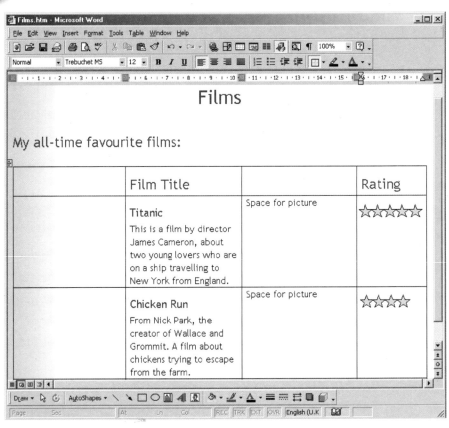

Figure 5.7 The Films Web page so far

Splitting Cells

Look back at Figure 5.1. It looks as though it is made up of a box containing hyperlinks (the navigation bar) on the left and an unconnected table of three columns on the right. In fact, it is a 5-column table with some of the cell borders hidden.

The table you are presently working on contains 4 columns. The first column can be split into two to make an extra column.

 Select column one by clicking just above its top border. (You will see the cursor change to a downward-pointing arrow.)

 From the Table menu, select Split Cells.

 In the dialogue box, select 2 columns and 4 rows and click OK.

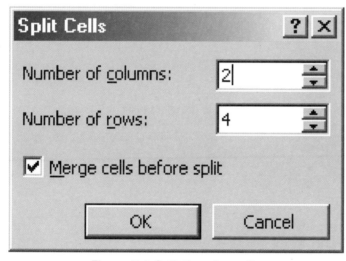

Figure 5.8 Splitting the cells

Removing cell borders

The borders need to be removed from the right half of this split column.

 Select what is now the second column.

 From the Format menu, select Borders and Shading.

Tip:
This is just one way of making an extra column. Alternatively, you could use **Table, Insert, Column** to insert an extra column!

Click the Borders tab at the top of the dialogue box.

 In the Preview box, click on the horizontal lines to remove them as shown in Figure 5.9 below.

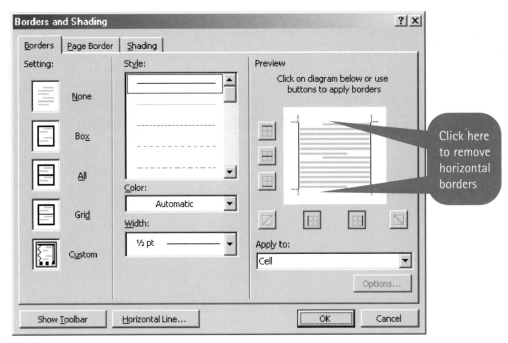

Figure 5.9: Removing borders

Now your page looks like this:

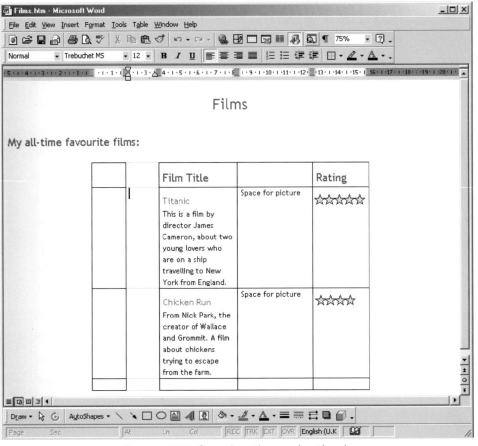

Figure 5.10: Creating the navigation bar

Inserting Hyperlinks

The hyperlinks will be put in the first column.

 Type the names of the other pages in the second cell of the first column. Insert some blank lines to space them out evenly.

 Highlight each page name and select Hyperlink from the Style box.

Figure 5.11: The Style box

Create a hyperlink to the appropriate page as follows:

 Highlight the first hyperlink, Home, and select Hyperlink from the Insert menu.

 In the Insert Hyperlink dialogue box, type default.htm in the text box labelled Type the file or Web page name.

 Similarly create hyperlinks for the other two, typing in the file name Music.htm for the Music page, and Sport.htm for the Sport page.

Smartening up

From here on, it's just a matter of deciding on how to make the page look really good. For a start, there are still a few extra empty cells that need to vanish.

We can make them invisible by deleting the borders in the first column from all the cells except the one containing the hyperlinks.

 Select the cells in the first column.

 Remove the borders by selecting None on the left of the Borders and Shading dialogue box as shown in Figure 5.9 above.

 Highlight the cell containing the hyperlinks. To do this, position the cursor at the bottom left corner of the cell. When it changes to a diagonal arrow, click.

 From the Format menu, select Borders and Shading.

 Click the Borders tab and select Box from the list of Setting pictures on the left of the screen. (See Figure 5.9.)

 Click OK.

Tip:
To select all the cells in a column, either drag across them or click just above the top row when the cursor is a downward pointing arrow.

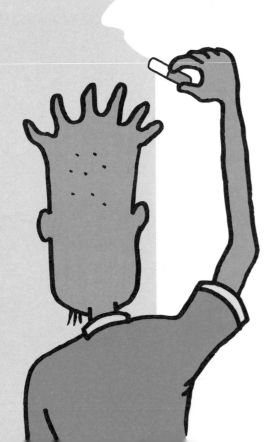

Terry's enthusiasm for deleting borders has just gone too far... Oi! Leave our tasteful tint panel alone!

Shading the navigation bar

You might decide that the Navigation bar would look better shaded a tasteful pale lavender or yellow.

 Go back into Borders and Shading.

 Click the Shading tab at the top of the dialogue box.

 Select a colour and click OK.

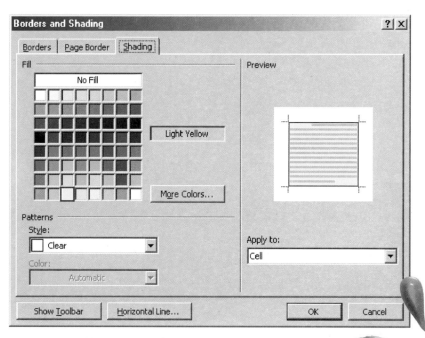

Figure 5.12: Shading the navigation bar

Your Films Web page should now look something like Figure 5.1.

 Save the page.

 Select Web Page Preview from the File menu to test your page including the hyperlinks.

 Close the Web Page Preview, and the Word document.

Chapter 6
Inserting Pictures

As you will have seen when you were exploring other Web sites in Chapter 1, Web pages contain not only text, but also pictures and sometimes other forms of media such as sound, animation and video clips.

Inserting Pictures

You can insert pictures from a number of different sources including:

 The Internet

 CD-ROMs

 Scanner

 Digital camera

Pictures can be stored on computers in different formats. You know which format a picture is stored in by the three-character suffix added to the end of the filename. A common picture format is bitmap, in which case .bmp is added to the end of the filename.

The problem with dealing with pictures on the WWW is that Web browsers can only view certain picture formats. However, fortunately Word will usually convert any picture you insert to GIF or JPG format which normally look fine on Web pages.

Finding suitable pictures

The Films Web page will have pictures from the various films mentioned displayed in the table. You could use a search engine to find some sites that have pictures from the films, or download the ones used in this example from the Payne-Gallway Web site (www.payne-gallway.co.uk/basicwebpages).

 Connect to the Internet.

 In the Address box type the address of your favourite search engine (e.g. www.yahoo.com).

 Search for Titanic (or whichever film you have chosen).

 Read the descriptions of the different pages, and find one which includes pictures.

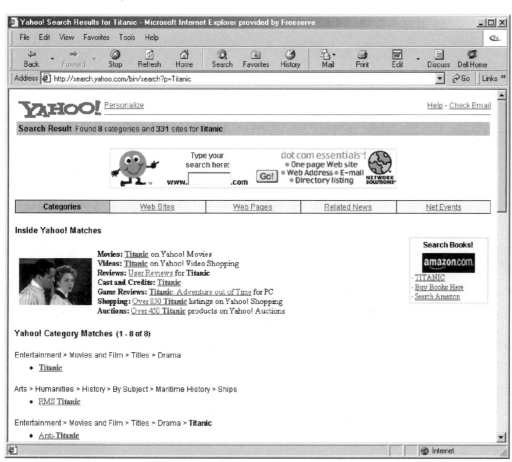

Figure 6.1: The search engine Yahoo

When you have found a suitable picture, right-click on it and select Save Picture As.

 Find the folder Films_Files, which was automatically formed by Word when you created the Films page. It will be a subfolder of the Web Site folder.

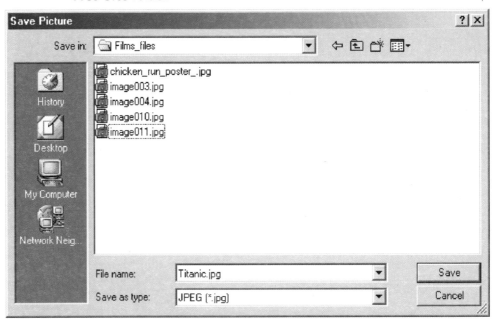

Figure 6.2: Saving the picture

Tip:

To disconnect, right-click the Dial-up icon in the Task Bar at the bottom right of the screen and select **Disconnect**.

 Choose a suitable filename (e.g. Titanic) and click OK.

Follow the same steps to find and save pictures for the other films.

Then log off the Internet and disconnect.

Terry was reluctantly pressganged into Emma's Leonardo DiCaprio fantasy...

Inserting pictures

▶ Load Word and open the document Films.htm.

▶ In the table, select the first cell that will contain a picture and delete the text Space for Picture.

▶ From the Insert menu select Picture, From File.

▶ In the Insert Picture dialogue box find the location of your picture.

▶ Click on the filename and click Insert.

▶ Size the picture by dragging the 'handles' around the outside border of the picture.

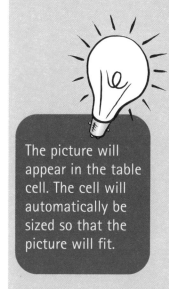

The picture will appear in the table cell. The cell will automatically be sized so that the picture will fit.

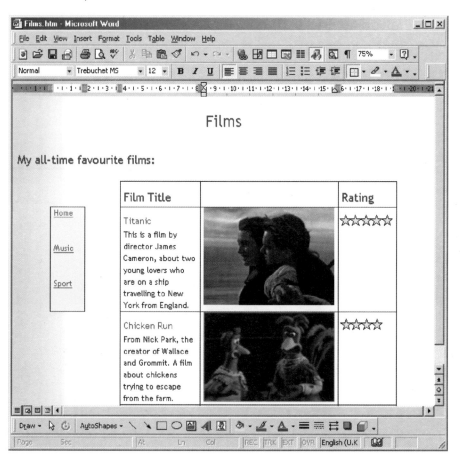

Figure 6.3: The pictures inserted into the Films Web page

Tip:
Save the Web page and preview it by selecting **Web Page Preview** from the **File** menu.

▶ Repeat the process to insert the pictures from the other films.

The Picture toolbar

When a picture is inserted into a Word document, the Picture toolbar usually appears. This toolbar is useful for specifying how you want text to wrap round an image, as well as controlling the image's contrast, brightness and size. The Crop button allows you to cut part of the picture off.

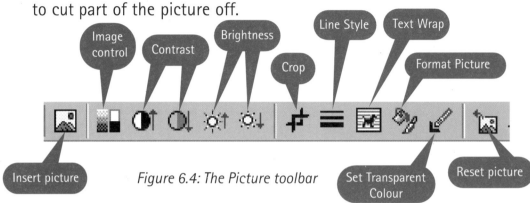

Figure 6.4: The Picture toolbar

Some people who browse the WWW use older types of browser and will not be able to see your pictures. You can insert a text description of your images that will be displayed as an alternative to seeing the picture.

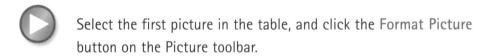 Select the first picture in the table, and click the Format Picture button on the Picture toolbar.

 Click the Web tab on the Format Picture dialogue box.

 Type your description in the box and click OK.

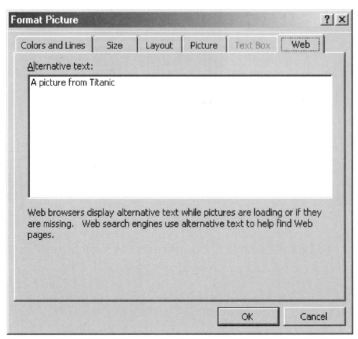

Figure 6.5: Entering alternative text

Inserting Clip Art

You can also insert Clip Art pictures that are supplied with Word 2000. You can either insert the pictures into a cell in the existing table or simply insert them anywhere on the page. The problem with doing this is that you will find, when you preview the Web page, the pictures have moved from where you put them!

We will anchor the pictures by inserting them into the table.

 Click in the cell above the Titanic picture.

 From the Insert menu select Picture, Clip Art.

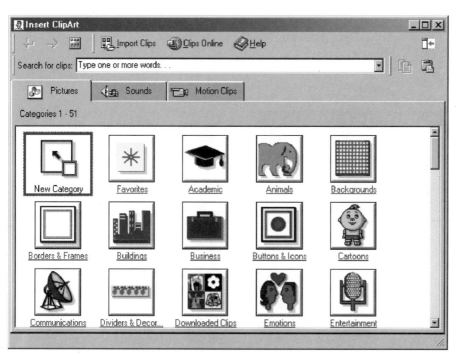

Figure 6.6: The ClipArt Gallery

 Select the Entertainment category and find an appropriate picture.

 Right-click and select Insert.

Inserting an animated picture

The Clip Art gallery also has some animated GIF format pictures that you can insert into your Web pages.

 Click in the cell above the navigation bar (the first cell in the table).

 From the Insert menu select Picture, Clip Art.

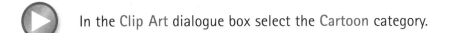 In the Clip Art dialogue box select the Cartoon category.

 Click on the Motion Clips tab.

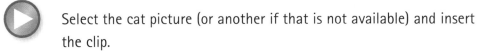 Select the cat picture (or another if that is not available) and insert the clip.

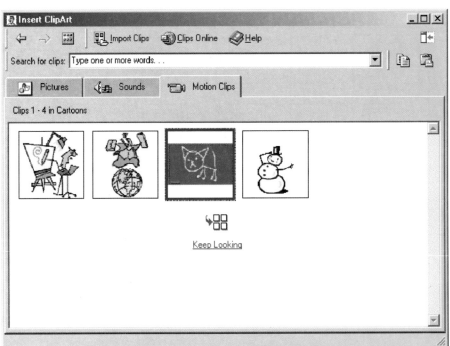

Figure 6.7: Inserting an animated picture

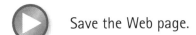 Size the picture appropriately in the cell.

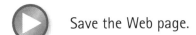 Save the Web page.

 Test the animation out by selecting Web Page Preview from the File menu.

Downloading more Clip Art and animated GIF files

You will find that many of the pictures in the Clip Art gallery are not stored on your computer. You will need the CD that was used to install Word 2000 to insert them into your Web page.

You can also access the Microsoft Web site and download lots more pictures and animated GIF files onto your computer. Remember though, images can take up a lot of space on your hard disk drive!

 From the Clip Art dialogue box, click on Clips Online.

You will automatically be connected to the Microsoft Web site. You can browse through their images and choose to download those you want. They will be stored in the Download category in the Clip Art dialogue box.

 Save and close when you have finished.

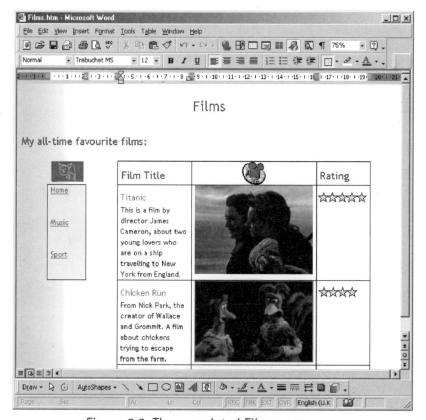

Figure 6.8: The completed Films page

Chapter 7
Inserting Multimedia

Now that you have completed the Films page, it's time to get to work on the other two, Music and Sport. We are going to use different types of Multimedia to enhance these two pages. You will be inserting sounds and scrolling text.

 Load Word and open the three Web pages, Music.htm, Sport.htm and Films.htm.

Copying and pasting the table to the Music page

You need to set up the table and navigation bar on the Music and Sport pages. It is similar in structure to the one you created on the Films page, so it can be copied and then edited.

 In Films.htm click anywhere in the table and from the Table menu, click Select, Table.

 Click Edit, Copy.

 Move to Music.htm and press Enter twice after the heading to leave a blank line.

 Click Edit, Paste Cells to paste the table to the Music page.

...and of course on Terry's web site, music by Bongo Ted will be heavily featured!

Adjusting the hyperlinks

▶ Delete the content from the three right-hand columns, leaving you with just the navigation bar completed.

▶ Delete the hyperlink Music and replace it with a hyperlink to the Films page.

▶ Do the same on the Sport page, but this time replace the hyperlink Sport with a hyperlink to the Films page.

Tip:
To insert the hyperlink click **Hyperlink** from the **Insert** menu and select the **Films.htm** file.

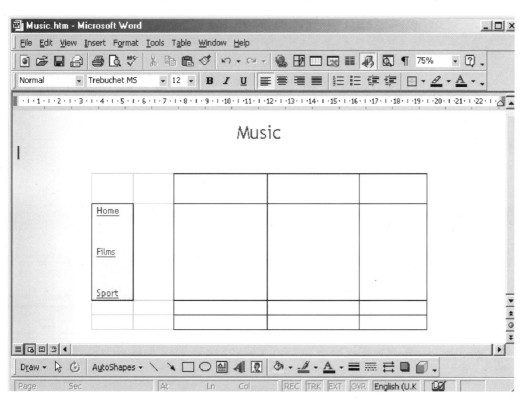

Figure 7.1: The new Music page

Linking to sound files

You can insert a hyperlink to a sound file, which people can click on to hear your favourite music. You can do this by linking to a file either on the Internet or on your local hard drive.

We will link to two midi sequence sound files that are provided with Microsoft Office and therefore stored on the hard drive of the computer.

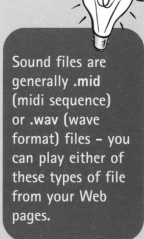

Sound files are generally **.mid** (midi sequence) or **.wav** (wave format) files – you can play either of these types of file from your Web pages.

First of all, type the text!

Before you insert the hyperlinks to the sound files, you need some text in the table.

 In the new table on the Music page, type the heading Band at the top of column two, Track at the top of column three and Audio at the top of column four.

 In the Band column, type Bongo Ted in one cell, and Jazzman Joe in the other.

 In the Track column, type Energetic in the cell next to Bongo Ted, and type Jazzy in the cell next to Jazzman Joe.

 In the Audio column, next to Energetic, type Click here to listen to Energetic.

 Type Click here to listen to Jazzy next to Jazzy.

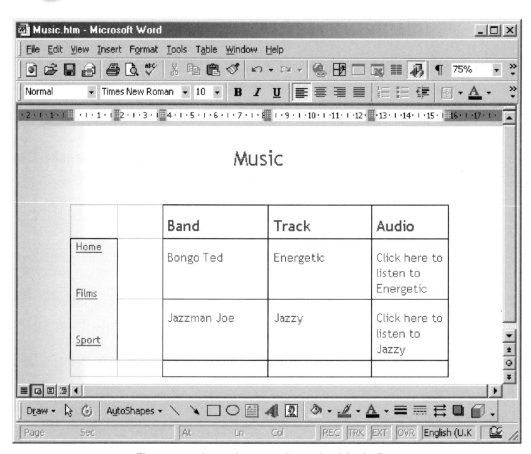

Figure 7.2: Inserting text into the Music Page

Making the Links

 Highlight the text Click here to listen to Energetic.

 Click the Insert Hyperlink button on the Standard toolbar.

 In the address box, type: C:\Program Files\Microsoft Office\Clipart\Pub60cor\sumer_01.mid and click OK.

 Now highlight the text Click here to listen to Jazzy.

 Click the Insert Hyperlink button on the Standard toolbar.

In the address box, type: C:\Program Files\Microsoft Office\Clipart\Pub60cor\Nbook_01.mid and click OK.

Save your work.

Test the sounds out by selecting Web Page Preview from the File menu and clicking on the hyperlinks.

Inserting a background sound

You can also link to sound files that will play when you open a Web page.

In Figure 7.3 below you will see the Web Tools toolbar, which you can display by clicking View, Toolbars.

The Insert Background Sound button allows you to link to a file in a similar way as you have done above, but this time you do not need to click on anything, it will play automatically.

Insert scrolling text

You may have seen a line of scrolling text (sometimes called a marquee) on other Web pages that you have visited while browsing the WWW. This feature can help draw attention to your page.

 On the Sport page click on a line underneath the main heading and above the table.

 On the Web Tools toolbar click the Scrolling Text button.

If the Web Tools toolbar is not displayed select **Toolbars, Web Tools** from the **View** menu.

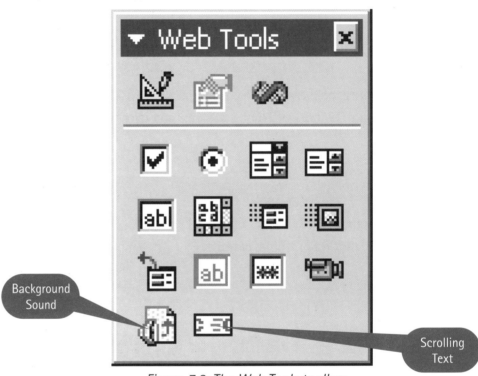

Background Sound

Scrolling Text

Figure 7.3: The Web Tools toolbar

Robin took his Scrolling Text for a spin around the block - with Fee in hot pursuit...

In the scrolling text dialogue box type Some of my sporting heroes in the middle box.

 Choose the type of behaviour, direction, speed and background colour you want. (Leave the loop option as infinite). Click OK.

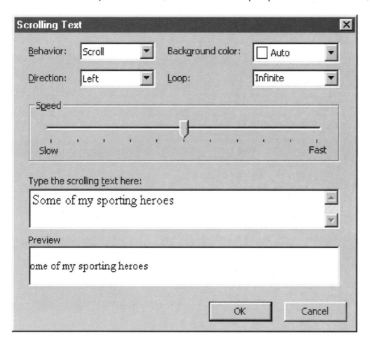

Figure 7.4: Inserting scrolling text

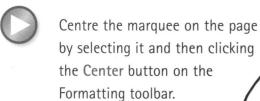 Back on the Web page, change the style, size and colour of the text. (You can stop the text scrolling by right-clicking it and pressing Stop).

 Centre the marquee on the page by selecting it and then clicking the Center button on the Formatting toolbar.

Save the Web page.

Terry developed a keen interest in tennis - only after he'd seen Anna Kournikova!

Finishing the page

 Complete the Sport page. Use the instructions given in Chapter 6 to insert some pictures of your favourite sporting heroes. You could find these pictures on the Internet or scan them in from Sports magazines that you may have.

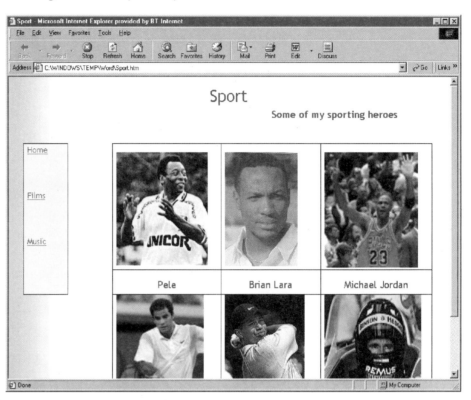

Figure 7.5: The completed Sports Page

Make sure you save the completed Sport page. Your four pages should now be complete.

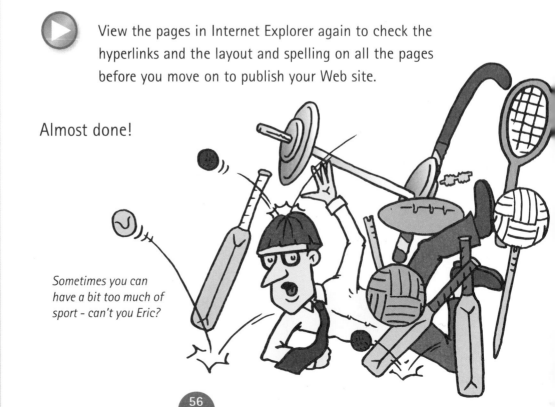 View the pages in Internet Explorer again to check the hyperlinks and the layout and spelling on all the pages before you move on to publish your Web site.

Almost done!

Sometimes you can have a bit too much of sport - can't you Eric?

Chapter 8
Publishing your Web Pages

Once you have created all the pages for your Web site and tested them, you are ready to publish them for all to see!

If you are working on a school network you may be able to publish your pages to the school Intranet. This means that everyone else on the network will be able to view your pages. Your teacher or network administrator can give you information on how to go about this.

If you want to publish your pages on the World Wide Web then you need to find a Web Site Hosting Company (a Web server) that will provide you with some Web space, a URL (Web site address), a username and password. You also need a method of transferring your files to the Web space. Two methods are shown here – using a Web folder and using FTP software.

Tip:
You must have an e-mail account before you can sign up for a Web account. If you haven't got one, go to **www.hotmail.com** and sign up for one.

Signing up for a Web account

This is the first step. There are several Web site hosting companies that let you publish Office 2000 Web pages directly to the Internet. Some of these companies offer this service free of charge, but you will find that advertisements will automatically appear on your site. (This is how they make their money!) Some of the companies that offer a free service are listed below:

Yahoo! GeoCities
(http://geocities.yahoo.com)

Angelfire
(http://angelfire.lycos.com)

Tripod
(http://www.tripod.lycos.com)

Talk City
(http://www.talkcity.com)

All of the sites mentioned give you step-by-step instructions. We will use Tripod as an example.

 Log on to www.tripod.lycos.com

 Click on Sign up.

 Fill in the sign-up form (take careful note of your member name). Terry's member name is terryssite.

 Submit the form.

Caution:

Web site hosting companies often change their procedures, so this could be different when you come to do it!

Your password will be e-mailed to you. This normally happens quickly, but it can take up to 48 hours!

Your Web site address will be:

http://members.tripod.com/<membername>/default.html

So, for example Terry's Web site address will be:

http://members.tripod.com/terryssite/default.html

You need to be connected to the Internet for the next step, which is to transfer the Web page files to the Web server either by creating a Web folder or by using FTP software, supported free by most Web hosting companies.

Create a Web folder

A Web folder is a shortcut from Word to a folder on your Web server. With Web folders you can save information directly to a Web server on the Internet or a local intranet.

 On the Windows desktop, double-click My Computer.

Double-click the Web Folders icon (or, if you have Microsoft Windows 2000, double-click My Network Places or Network Neighbourhood).

 Double-click the Add Web Folders icon (or, if you have Microsoft Windows 2000, double-click Add Network Place).

Figure 8.1: Displaying the Web folders

 In the Type the Location to Add field, type your Web site address: http://members.tripod.com/<membername>

Figure 8.2: Entering the Web folder location

Click Next.

At this point you may have to wait a while – be patient!!

In the Enter Network Password dialogue box, type the member name (user name) and password that you used to sign up for your Web account.

 Click OK.

 In the Add Web Folder dialogue box, type a name for this Web folder or accept the one it gives you e.g. terryssite on members. tripod.com.

Figure 8.3: Naming the Web folder

 Click Finish.

In My Computer you will now see the new Web folder that has been created.

Figure 8.4: The new Web folder

You must now transfer the Web pages to the host Web server by transferring the files you created in the previous chapters to your new Web folder (e.g. terryssite on members.tripod.com). You still need to be connected to the Internet.

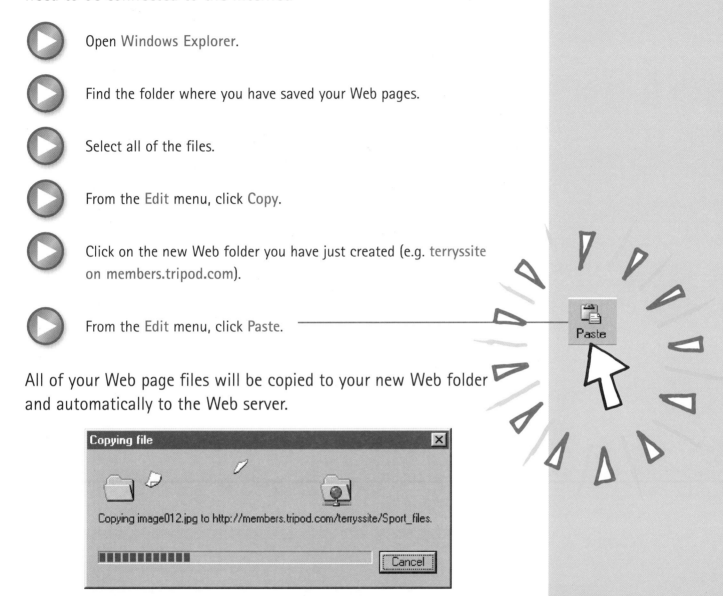

Open Windows Explorer.

Find the folder where you have saved your Web pages.

Select all of the files.

From the Edit menu, click Copy.

Click on the new Web folder you have just created (e.g. terryssite on members.tripod.com).

From the Edit menu, click Paste.

All of your Web page files will be copied to your new Web folder and automatically to the Web server.

Figure 8.5: Copying the files to the Web folder and the Web server

When the copying process has finished your Web pages should be loaded on the Web server.

Transferring your files using FTP

Sometimes creating a Web folder can take a very long time, so an alternative method is to transfer your files using FTP (File Transfer Protocol) software provided by the hosting company. This sounds complicated, but it isn't.

▶ Open Internet Explorer.

▶ In the Address box type the following
ftp://membername:password@ftp.tripod.com

▶ Remember in Terry's case his member name was terryssite. (He's not telling you what his password is!)

You will be connected to your Web space.

▶ Open Windows Explorer so that you can see your Web page files on your local disk.

▶ Drag the files across into Internet Explorer to copy them into your Web space.

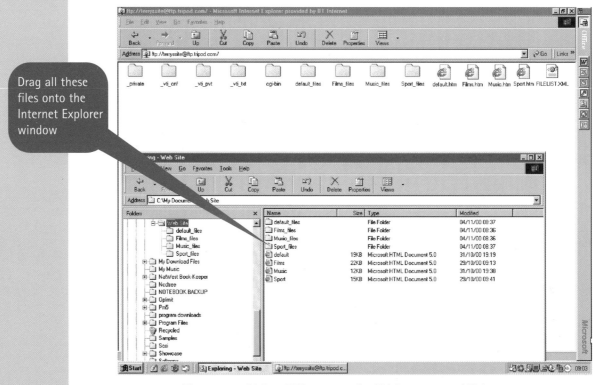

Figure 8.6: Using FTP to transfer Web pages to Web server

Check it out!

 In Internet Explorer enter the address of your home page
(e.g. http://members.tripod.com/terryssite/default.htm)

 Your home page should be displayed. Congratulations!

 Test the links to your other three pages, the links to other sites
from your home page and the links to the sound files.

 Check that all the pictures are displayed and do not take too long to load.

Don't forget that the Web hosting company will place some adverts
on your pages, like you can see on Terry's home page below – there's
not much you can do about that.

Now you can tell all your friends your Web site address!

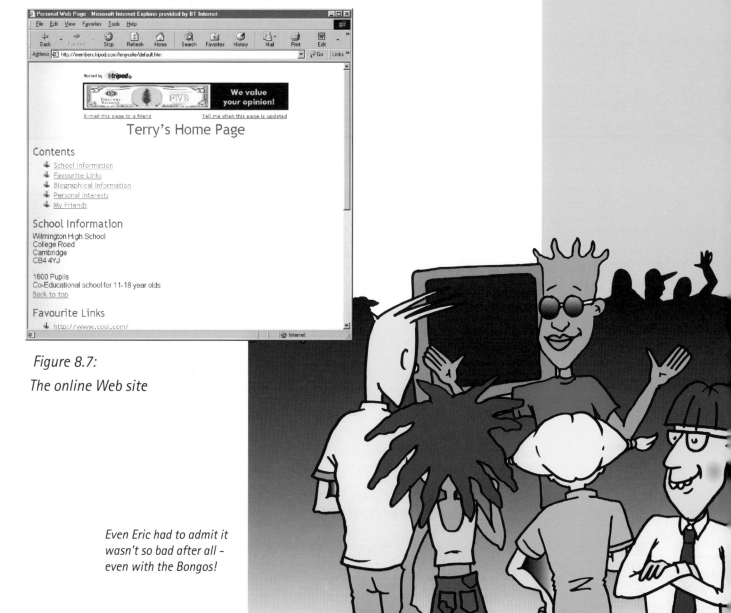

Figure 8.7:
The online Web site

*Even Eric had to admit it
wasn't so bad after all –
even with the Bongos!*

Index